I0210792

CHERL L. ROBINSON

TAKING CONTROL

OF YOUR

FINANCIAL

FUTURE

GOD'S WAY

"The framework for your financial destiny"

FOREWORD BY APOSTLE KIMBERLY JONES

Copyright @ 2024 by Cherl L Robinson

www.financegodsway.com

ISBN: 978-1-953788-98-6

Published by Beyond the Book Media, LLC

Alpharetta, Georgia

www.beyondthebookmedia.com

All rights reserved solely by Author. No part of this publication may be reproduced, distributed, or transmitted in any form or by any means, including photocopying, recording, or other electronic or mechanical methods, without the prior written permission of the author, except in the case of brief quotations embodied in critical reviews and certain other noncommercial uses permitted by copyright law. For permission requests, email to the author at cherl.robinson@financegodsway.com. Limit of Liability/Disclaimer of Warranty: While the publisher and author have used their best efforts in preparing this book, they make no representations of warranties with respect to the accuracy or completeness of the contents of this book and specifically disclaim any implied warranties or merchantability or fitness for a particular purpose. No warranty may be created or extended by sales representatives or written sales materials. The advice and strategies contained herein may not be suitable for your situation. You should consult with a professional where appropriate. Neither the publisher nor author shall be liable for damages arising here from.

All quoted scriptures are taken from King James Version Bible, unless otherwise indicated: *AMP – Amplified Bible, NIV – New International Version, NKJV - New King James Version, or NLT – New Living Translation.*

Dedication

I dedicate this book to my husband, the love of my life,

Lemiah Robinson.

Thank you for your love and encouragement.

Thank you for always being in my corner, gently pushing

me forward so that I can do anything.

Honey,

I will always love and cherish you.

Table of Contents

Foreword

"The Lord will perfect that which concerneth me: thy mercy, O Lord endureth forever: forsake not the works of thine own hands." (Psalm 138:8)

Psalm 138:8 speaks of God perfecting those things concerning His people. Upon surface investigation of this scripture and the word "perfect," we might infer that God has the intent of making us to be perfect in the sense of having no flaws or shortcomings. But the truth of the matter, is that this is not what this scripture is suggesting at all.

Based upon its original Hebrew meaning, *"perfect"* is associated with maturation and completion. In essence, this means that God is bringing those things concerning us into full maturity with nothing missing or broken. I truly believe that God's desire is to perfect us in every area of our lives.

God is concerned about us from a holistic perspective. People of faith will readily agree that God wants to equip us and bring us into full maturity as it pertains to our walk with Him, our relationships with others, and our fulfillment of purpose. However, when it comes to the area of our finances, we seem to think that our fiscal perfection is of little, or no concern to God. This could be no further from the truth.

In Taking Control of Your Financial Future God's Way, Cherl Robinson champions the cause of correcting erroneous and irresponsible thinking as it pertains to the relationship between the Christian faith and finances. These two constructs are not as far away from one another as many may believe. God is concerned about the state of our financial posture. When we are handicapped in the area of financial fortitude, we are hindered in our faith.

As the Word of God asserts, money truly does answer all things. As you read this book, listen for the answers to the questions you have been asking and the challenges you have been facing in the area of financial stewardship. You will discover innumerable gems of revelation couched within the pages of this amazing book. As you read through each chapter, prepare yourself for a greater level of understanding and equipping for taking authority over your financial future God's way.

Apostle Kimberly Jones
For His Glory Global, Inc.

Preface

This book is not meant to be another book about finances.

This is a book meant to bring awareness to the outside forces that impede your financial progress and, in many cases, alter your financial destiny.

God desires that we prosper and live abundant lives!

Acknowledgments

To every Pastor, Ministry Leader, or Woman of God
who has poured into my life.
I say, thank you.
Your labor of love has not been in vain.

Apostles Louis and Kimberly Jones
Pastor Vorlea Chaney
Dr. Nancy Joy Dozier
Pastor Rachel Senior
Pastor James J. Minnick
Apostle Frankie H. Young
Pastors Michael and Brenda Jones
Bishop Andrew Merritt
Bishop Keith Butler
Dr. Mildred C. Harris

Special thank you to my nephew and niece in love,
Rev. Hercules and Deborah Bobian

Introduction

Taking control of your financial future God's way is more than just creating a budget and sticking with it or obtaining a savings account. It is all-inclusive of your entire financial make-up, everything that affects you financially. It is often the unseen things that affect us financially that cause us to lose control of our financial future. Just as we have life goals and pursuits for our future, other things can take us off course; and create a future for us that we may not desire.

It is this "happenstance future" that perpetuates poverty in our lives or causes us to become impoverished. When I say it causes "poverty" or to live an impoverished lifestyle, I am referring to "the struggle," where you find yourself always having to struggle to get by, work one to two jobs just to try to live somewhat comfortably.

Yet, there is another group of people that seem to never struggle or must work several jobs just to get by, even if they are making relatively the same income as you. What's up with that? The difference, as a people, they have taken control of their economic destiny.

My father used to always make comparisons between White and Black people as it related to their economic success and prosperity. Initially, I found his constant comparison to be annoying, but when I began to listen, it made sense. What my father was saying was, "Pay attention to what those who are successful are doing, then imitate what they have done."

In my career, most positions I have held were in departments where I was the only Black person. Through this, I have learned many lessons, one of my first as a bank teller. I learned that when a child is born, the parent or grandparent, would open a savings account to prepare for that child to go to college. Deposits to this account would become a part of the household budget. If the child were a girl, a separate account would be established, to save for her wedding. They left nothing to chance. It was expected for their child to go to college, and it was expected that their girls would also marry.

In the Black community, when a child is born, he/she is welcomed with love, clothes, toys, and well wishes. No accounts are established. In most cases, the parents will rely upon governmental grants or loan programs to fund their child's college education. In some cases, the child is left to fend for themselves where higher-level educational expenses are concerned. There are no separate accounts set up for their daughter's preparation for marriage. Although college and marriage may be internal desires for Black parents for their children, most do nothing to prepare or set it in motion, which is a recipe for disaster.

When I graduated from high school, government grants were readily available for most African Americans, because most came from humble beginnings. I remember one of my college advisors admonishing students to make the most of the grant money because it would not always be around. I later found this to be true. While I was a freshman and sophomore, financial aid was readily available. When I became a junior, I was soon met with my financial aid being cut almost fifty percent for no apparent reason. My financial status had not changed, nor had the status of my family. I saw many of my friends would have to drop out of school because they could not finance the costs, and most of us received no help from our families. This lack of financial support resulted in several years of delay in receiving my bachelor's degree, but praise be unto God, I did not let that stop me.

I initially attended a college located in a small rural area of Michigan. The town had two grocery stores, two banks, and one major retailer. I was blessed to be one of the only Black students employed within the town. I worked for one of the local banks, and another Black student worked at a known fast-food establishment as a supervisor. We were the exceptions, as the other Black students worked in the cafeteria at the college. This may sound privileged, but it wasn't. I only made enough money to barely get by. In fact, my hours were so dim and closely monitored that they were only enough for me to make my weekly rent payments. While struggling to educate myself, I fasted often, mostly out of necessity, due to a lack of funds and no financial support from my family.

Once my situation had become so dire, I reached out to my grandmother for help. I asked her if she would send me thirty dollars for food. I explained to her my urgency, and she agreed to send the funds immediately. After two days, I walked the four miles to the post office, and there was nothing. The next day, it was the same thing. On the fourth day, still nothing from my grandmother, but God showed up on my behalf and provided a check from the local utility company in the amount of $30. What my family lacked in support for me, God provided. As I testified of God's goodness others began to pour financially into me. Even one of the church families, who were farmers, adopted me, so to speak. They would have me over for dinner and provide me with vegetables from their garden. May the blessings of God always be with them and their memory.

You may be wondering what happened to the money my grandmother was supposed to have sent. After checking with the post office on the fourth day, I called my grandmother to see what happened. I was told that she had to buy her pastor a dining room suite. What a case of misplaced priority! Here is your granddaughter literally starving and asking for your help. You agree to help her, but instead spend all your money buying your pastor a dining room suite, leaving your granddaughter to starve to death. Misplaced priority, where is the blessing in that? You can't help her with thirty dollars, but you can spend several thousand dollars purchasing a dining room suite for your pastor.

Sometimes, we experience financial hardship because we give priority to the wrong thing. Misplaced priority is defined as importance directed towards someone or something wrongly or in a way that does not show good judgment. I am not saying that the church or the man or woman of God in our lives is not important. I am not saying that we should not hold them in high esteem. However, there is a divine order for all things, and our priorities should be properly aligned:

- God

- Marriage

- Family

- Church

Yes, we are to love and respect the man and woman of God in our lives, but it should not be at the expense of our families.

Chapter One

First Things First

"The earth is the Lord's, and the fulness thereof, the world and they that dwell therein." *(Psalms 24:1)*

First things first, all wealth comes from God. All the silver, all the gold belongs to Him. The Bible says, "The earth is the Lord's, and the fulness thereof, the world and they that dwell therein." So, everything belongs to God! This includes our paycheck. Nothing we own belongs to us. We are only caretakers (stewards) of God's financial resources. As God's caretakers, we must realize that everything we have in our possession is a result of His allowing us to manage His treasury and that according to our ability to manage.

> [14]"Again, it will be like a man going on a journey, who called his servants and entrusted his wealth to them. [15] To one he gave five bags of gold, to another two bags, and to another one bag,[a] each according to his ability. Then he went on his journey. [16] The man who had received five bags of gold went at once and put his money to work and gained five bags more. [17] So also, the one with two bags of gold gained two more. [18] But the man who had received

one bag went off, dug a hole in the ground and hid his master's money." *(Matthew 25:14-18 NIV)*

The servants listed in this parable are actual stewards or caretakers of what was entrusted to them. Note, the two servants who were successful. The scripture says that they immediately employed their master's money. This may have been some investment or business opportunity. At any time, when we are working with finances, we must keep proper records. We must make sure that the bills are paid on time as agreed with our creditors, and we must take careful thought as to what opportunities we pursue and count the cost.

I used to wonder about this parable; my mind was always curious as to the last servant, who was unsuccessful. He received a bag of money from his master and buried it. He was certain to return to his master what was given to him. What was so wrong with that? I did not realize that it was the wicked servant's attitude that got him in trouble; he was careful NOT to prosper. The other two servants were wise, and acted as their Master would have if he were present.

When I grew up, I can recall a couple family members who were not necessarily good money managers. They would ask my grandmother to keep money for them to prevent them from spending it. After a while, they would return, and she always had their money. Now, I do not know if they received interest or anything. I always believed that she just held it, without spending it. So, this was always intriguing to me. They did not expect my grandmother to invest their money, but what if she did? What if, when they returned, instead of receiving $500, she gave them $1,000 because she was able to double their money? I am sure this would have been welcomed with joy, and more would have been entrusted to her.

[19] "After a long time the master of those servants returned and settled accounts with them.[20] The man who had received five bags of gold brought the other five. 'Master,' he said, 'you entrusted me with five bags of gold. See, I have gained five more.'[21] "His master replied, 'Well done, good and faithful servant! You have been faithful with a few things; I will put you in charge of many things. Come and share your master's happiness!'[22] "The man with two bags of gold also came. 'Master,' he said, 'you entrusted me with two bags of gold; see, I have gained two more.'[23] "His master replied, 'Well done, good and faithful servant! You have been faithful with a few things; I will put you in charge of many things. Come and share your master's happiness!'[24] "Then the man who had received one bag of gold came. 'Master,' he said, 'I knew that you are a hard man, harvesting where you have not sown and gathering where you have not scattered seed.[25] So I was afraid and went out and hid your gold in the ground. See, here is what belongs to you.'[26] "His master replied, 'You wicked, lazy servant! So you knew that I harvest where I have not sown and gather where I have not scattered seed?[27] Well

then, you should have put my money on deposit with the bankers, so that when I returned I would have received it back with interest.[28] "So take the bag of gold from him and give it to the one who has ten bags.[29] For whoever has will be given more, and they will have an abundance. Whoever does not have, even what they have will be taken from them." *(Matthew 25:19-29 NIV)*

In the scripture, each servant was given according to his ability. Each person is different. We all come from different backgrounds; therefore, we more than likely would encounter different opportunities. One person may have a Ph.D. and another a high school diploma, but each made a steward according to their ability to manage. It is how we manage what we do with the money entrusted in our care that makes the difference.

God has entrusted his wealth to us, and we must give an account of how we managed his resources. Did we increase God's wealth? Or did God's wealth decline under our watch? Or did it just lie dormant? Learning to take control of our financial future, God's way, will ultimately set us up for God to say, "Well done, good and faithful servant."

Get Organized

Now that we have acknowledged that all things belong to God, our next step in taking control of our financial future is to get organized. When the financial home is out of order or filled with clutter, it breeds chaos and confusion. You can't find anything, and worse, you have no clue what's going on with your bank account. It is during this stage of disorganization that bank overdrafts, non-sufficient fund (NSF) checks, and bank charges occur.

These bank charges result in more debt and frustration for the individual and can easily get out of control. Many times, the individual will become so frustrated and overwhelmed that they misplace the blame of their bank errors onto the organizations they asked to debit their accounts; instead of blaming themselves for not properly balancing their checkbook and making sure that funds were available to cover their preauthorized transactions.

> "Be diligent to know the condition of your flocks
> and pay attention to your herds; for riches are not
> forever, nor does a crown endure to all generations."
> *(Proverbs 27:23-24 AMP)*

The Bible is very clear about us knowing our financial condition; and being intentional about our finances. Therefore, we must take an honest look at our entire financial situation. We cannot begin any type of journey without first knowing the starting point, and this journey to taking control of our financial future is no different.

We must begin by taking a financial inventory of our financial life. Through this inventory, we will ascertain the equity position we have in our household, the amount of debt we owe, and the value of our assets, the things we own via a report called a statement of financial position.

Statement of Financial Position

The statement of financial position is considered a picture or snapshot of your financial house at a precise moment, which would be the date of the statement. We can learn a lot from it because it not only provides a listing of assets, liabilities, and net worth that depicts resources but also tells us how those resources were obtained or financed.

- Asset – property owned completely or partially by you.

- Liability – money you owe to creditors and individuals.

- Net worth – the amount of wealth or equity you have in owned assets. It is the amount of money that would remain after selling all your owned assets at their estimated fair market values and paying off your debts.

Let's make a list of your assets (everything you own) and record the current market values in a spreadsheet (see sample worksheet in appendix). You want to list the amount of cash you have on hand, in bank accounts, and in savings vehicles. List any money owed to you, that you honestly expect will be paid. List property values including residence, automobiles, coin/stamp collections, etc.

Now make a list of all your liabilities (debts) and record the balances on a spreadsheet. On a separate ledger, record the balance, monthly payment, interest rate, payment date, and number of remaining payments (see appendix for sample). This will include loan balances: automobile, credit cards, mortgages, taxes, education, etc.

Assets – Liabilities = Net Worth

After all asset values and liabilities have been listed on the worksheet, subtract the total asset value from the total liabilities. This will yield your net worth. Your net worth is the difference between total assets and total liabilities. A positive net worth is a great start to taking control of our financial future, but a negative net worth means that we are somewhat impoverished and will require our absolute attention.

Statement of Personal Cash Flow

The financial inventory will also capture how your money is being spent via a report called Statement of Personal Cash Flows. The Statement of Personal Cash Flow presents a summary of your income and expenses during the period. This statement will also show the amount of free money available for you to use at your discretion, making it easier for us to put things into perspective.

- Income – all monies you receive, in cash, from employment, investments, and other sources.

- Expenses – recurring obligations that you pay on a regular basis. It can be a monthly, quarterly, or annual expense. It can be a fixed amount, or the amounts can vary, i.e.— food, gasoline, telephone etc.

- Discretionary Cash Flow – money available after all expenses are accounted for and paid.

Income – Expenses = Discretionary Cash Flow

List all income sources and amounts on the income section of the worksheet. Then, you will want to account for every expense that you have, beginning with those that are currently due, and paid monthly. Then, record those expenses that are variable, where the billed amounts vary monthly, quarterly, or annually.

Looking at the statements, we can intentionally make decisions about the direction we desire our financial lives to take; and make necessary changes while setting goals for our future.

Establishing Goals

Our next step is to create a financial plan. Financial planning, according to the National Endowment for Financial Education, is a process of setting goals, developing a plan to achieve them, and putting the plan into action. It's creating a roadmap for handling everything you do with your money – spending, saving, using credit, and investing.

> "Where there is no vision, the people perish: but he that keepeth the law, happy is he." *(Proverbs 29:18)*

Setting financial goals is both practical and biblical. It is important to know what we want to accomplish in life, our dreams, or our vision for the future. If we have no vision for our future, we walk aimlessly and settle for whatever happens.

"Then the Lord answered me and said: "Write the vision and make it plain on tablets, that he may run who reads it. For the vision is yet for an appointed time; But at the end it will speak, and it will not lie. Though it tarries, wait for it; Because it will surely come, It will not tarry." *(Habakkuk 2:2-3 NKJV)*

When we write out our goals, create action plans, and work on them, we tend to stay on track in accomplishing our goals. Then, as we complete each goal, we can see how we begin to take control, and our future or destiny will begin to take shape in our dreams. Notice that just knowing what we want to accomplish and not doing anything to make it happen does not avail us of anything. We must work on our plans, applying action steps to bring them to pass. Nothing just happens.

I am sure you may have heard individuals in the church setting professing themselves to be millionaires. Well, that's a great confession, but what are they doing about it to make it happen? Most are doing nothing; they think it will just happen out of nowhere one day.

"Go to the ant, thou sluggard; consider her ways, and be wise: which having no guide, overseer, or ruler, provideth her meat in the summer, and gathereth her food in the harvest." *(Proverbs 6:6-8)*

Maybe God has called you to be a millionaire. If so, you must seek God to find His direct plan and purpose. Then, you must position yourself for this to take place. Let's say God showed you owning million-dollar real estate properties, which would bring you millionaire status. Then, in positioning yourself, you first need to learn about real estate and real estate investing. Read books, attend seminars, and watch TV shows dealing with real estate. Then, when the time is right, begin purchasing real estate projects and allow the Holy Spirit to direct your path. This is how you would position yourself for millionaire status in regard to real estate and open the door for God's opportunities to manifest in your life.

Now that we have identified our goals and measured them, we must look at our current financial situation. It is not enough for us to create a goal or know what we desire and when, without creating an action plan to obtain it.

Chapter Two

Breaking Free

"The Lord shall open unto thee his good treasure, the heaven to give the rain unto thy land in his season, and to bless all the work of thine hand: and **thou shalt lend unto many nations, and thou shalt not borrow.**" *(Deuteronomy 28:12)*

The will of God is that we be lenders and not borrowers. God desires that we be the head and not the tail, above and not beneath. You may ask, how can this be? Have you ever wondered how some people seem to be so great at handling money? They may have lower incomes but seem to accomplish so much. You ask, "What is the secret? What do they know that I don't?"

The answer lies in their obedience to God in financial matters. Please note, I am not speaking about their obedience to God in the giving of their finances. Yes, God has called us to be givers, and requires such, but He has much more to say about finances. It is when we tap into the wisdom of God and apply His financial principles and wisdom to our financial lives that we begin to thrive.

"And it shall come to pass, if thou shalt hearken diligently unto the voice of the Lord thy God, to observe and to do all his commandments which I command thee this day, that the Lord thy God will set thee on high above all nations of the earth:

2 And all these blessings shall come on thee, and overtake thee, if thou shalt hearken unto the voice of the Lord thy God.

3 Blessed shalt thou be in the city, and blessed shalt thou be in the field.

4 Blessed shall be the fruit of thy body, and the fruit of thy ground, and the fruit of thy cattle, the increase of thy kine, and the flocks of thy sheep.

5 Blessed shall be thy basket and thy store.

6 Blessed shalt thou be when thou comest in, and blessed shalt thou be when thou goest out.

7 The Lord shall cause thine enemies that rise up against thee to be smitten before thy face: they shall come out against thee one way, and flee before thee seven ways.

8 The Lord shall command the blessing upon thee in thy storehouses, and in all that thou settest thine

hand unto; and he shall bless thee in the land which the Lord thy God giveth thee.

9 The Lord shall establish thee an holy people unto himself, as he hath sworn unto thee, if thou shalt keep the commandments of the Lord thy God, and walk in his ways.

10 And all people of the earth shall see that thou art called by the name of the Lord; and they shall be afraid of thee.

11 And the Lord shall make thee plenteous in goods, in the fruit of thy body, and in the fruit of thy cattle, and in the fruit of thy ground, in the land which the Lord sware unto thy fathers to give thee.

12 The Lord shall open unto thee his good treasure, the heaven to give the rain unto thy land in his season, and to bless all the work of thine hand: and thou shalt lend unto many nations, and thou shalt not borrow.

13 And the Lord shall make thee the head, and not the tail; and thou shalt be above only, and thou shalt not be beneath; if that thou hearken unto the commandments of the Lord thy God, which I command thee this day, to observe and to do them:

¹⁴ And thou shalt not go aside from any of the words which I command thee this day, to the right hand, or to the left, to go after other gods to serve them."
(Deuteronomy 28:1-14)

God has much to say about our financial lives, but our response must be obedience to the wisdom of God. After all, it all belongs to Him. He will not lead us into a negative place. We must be intentional in giving attention to our finances, and our obedience to God.

If you have been struggling with debt and/or not enough to meet your needs. You work, and yet money seems to evaporate from your hands. You earn wages, but it seems like your money is spent before you can get home. You are robbing Peter to pay Paul. There seems to always be something that happens to keep you in a financial hole. You go from one financial struggle to the next. Consider your ways and your relationship to God. Could it be that sin has cursed you from prospering?

> "Will a man rob God? Yet ye have robbed me. But ye say, Wherein have we robbed thee? In tithes and offerings.
>
> ⁹ Ye are cursed with a curse: for ye have robbed me, even this whole nation.
>
> ¹⁰ Bring ye all the tithes into the storehouse, that there may be meat in mine house, and prove me now herewith, saith the Lord of hosts, if I will not open you the windows of heaven, and pour you out

a blessing, that there shall not be room enough to receive it.

11 And I will rebuke the devourer for your sakes, and he shall not destroy the fruits of your ground; neither shall your vine cast her fruit before the time in the field, saith the Lord of hosts.

12 And all nations shall call you blessed: for ye shall be a delightsome land, saith the Lord of hosts." *(Malachi 3:8-12)*

When we tithe, we break the curse, and God rebukes the devourer. We may never know everything God does behind the scenes for us, but He intervenes in our situation. Simply stated, he will cause blessings upon us. Notice, this is the only place in scripture, that I have found that God has told us to prove Him if he will not respond to His word. In fact, the Bible says that God watches over His word to perform it.

What is tithing? Simply put, tithing is the giving of ten percent of all that you receive to God. Remember, it all belongs to God. If we are not tithing the Bible says that we are thieves, because we are robbing God of what is His.

Tithing Facts:
- What? The tithe is Holy to God (Lev. 27:30).
- Whom? We give tithes unto God.
- Where? We tithe in the house of God (Church).
- Why? Tithing opens the windows of heaven over the tither.

- When? When we are faithful to tithe and give offerings, God will pour out His blessings upon us.

"A tithe of everything from the land, whether grain from the soil or fruit from the trees, belongs to the Lord; it is holy to the Lord." *(Leviticus 27:30 NIV)*

God is holy, and how we manage the holy things of God must be done with reverential respect. The first ten percent of our income earned, is considered holy by God. Therefore, we are to immediately set it aside so that the tithe is never comingled with regular ordinary funds.

Paper Check	1. Cash the payroll check and remove the tithe.
	2. Immediately purchase a cashier's check or money order payable to your local church.
	3. Then, worship God.
Electronic Deposit	1. Move tithe funds to a separate bank account.
	2. Request the employer to deposit up to 25% of your pay into a separate account for the tithe. The extra will help account for any gross deductions that should be included in the tithe calculation.
	3. Then, worship God

Note: The tithe comes out first before we begin any spending. We honor God when we revere His tithe.

Chapter Three

Putting Things in Order

"You have sown much, and bring in little; you eat, but do not have enough; you drink, but you are not filled with drink; you clothe yourselves, but no one is warm; **and he who earns wages, earns wages to put into a bag with holes.**" *(Haggai 1:6 NKJV)*

One of the most important things in taking control of your financial future God's way is gaining control of your spending. When we take control, we become intentional with our finances by coming out of debt and empowering our money to work for us, to create wealth and generational blessings.

It is important that we know where our money is going. Journal your daily purchases for a month to discover where money is going. Record anything you purchase in a journal for the month. Later, we will compare it with the target spending plan (budget) we will establish for ourselves. As we monitor our spending, we will be able to see where our money is going and in what areas adjustments may be made.

The Spending Plan (Budget)

The word "budget" over the years has received a bad reputation in that some people look upon it as a tool of deprivation. However, it is really a liberating tool because it helps to align finances in a way that everything is accounted for and brings peace of mind to financial matters. It places our finances under our intentional control.

The spending plan I recommend is simple, focusing on after-tax dollars, which allows you to account for your "needs and wants" while saving for the future and coming out of debt. It is the 50/30/20 rule.

50/30/20
Spending Plan

Needs (50% of after-tax pay)	Wants (30% of after-tax pay)	Savings & Debt Repayment (20% of after-tax pay)
Mandatory bills needed for your survival.	Things considered nice to have or do.	Anything towards your financial future
• Basic clothing • Childcare • Debts, minimum payments due • Food • Healthcare • Housing • Insurance • Transportation • Utilities	• Dining out • Entertainment • Hobbies • Junk food • Lifestyle Improvements • Memberships • Recreation • Spending sprees • Streaming services • Subscriptions	• Debts, above min due • Education • Investments • Retirement • Sp. Savings • Vacation

Let's build our target spending plan:

- Calculate your after-tax income – Add all sources of income, including employment wages, alimony, child support, rental income, side hustle, etc. – deduct tithe and all payroll withholdings.

- Calculate spending plan allocations based on the 50/30/20 split – Multiply your after-tax income by 50%, 30%, and 20% so that you may determine the amount of spending for each bucket, for example:

Net Income is $5,000

Needs	$5,000 (0.50)	$2,500
Wants	$5,000 (0.30)	$1,500
Savings & Repayment	$5,000 (0.20)	$1,000

- Now that we have determined what we should be spending, let's compare our category totals with our daily purchase journal introduced at the beginning of the chapter. Do not be alarmed if there is a gap between where you are and where you should be. Our spending plan is a target for us to aim at. Begin to adjust your spending so that you will get as close as possible to the goal of 50/30/20. If overspending is occurring in the needs category, you may need to downsize your lifestyle and consider more affordable options. Continue to monitor your spending and make the necessary adjustments; it may take a few months.

Debt Reduction/Payoff

> "Owe no man anything, but to love one another: for he that loveth another hath fulfilled the law." *(Romans 13:8 KJV)*

It is clear that God does not desire for us to be in debt. As we continue our journey in taking control of our financial future, God's way, we must become intentional in our spending and come out of debt. No more working for bags with holes in them, and no more debt. Devise a debt reduction strategy to pay off your debts. I recommend taking a snowball approach to your debt reduction payoff strategy. First, apply extra monies to pay off smaller debts, then the monies paid to smaller debts apply to larger debts along with their regular payment, giving priority to debt with higher interest rates.

Handling Financial Affairs

God desires that we be people of integrity, and we are to walk in integrity in all areas of our lives including how we handle His finances. People of integrity are honest, trustworthy, and exercise good, strong moral character. Integrity is not just about being honest in our words and actions but also fulfilling the responsibilities that we have been entrusted with. People of integrity are prompt in their commitments maintaining an attitude that pleases God. Integrity brings favor and blessing.

If we borrow $5 from a brother or sister and promise to repay them on Sunday. When Sunday comes, integrity repays the brother or sister their $5 regardless of what sowing opportunity may have been presented during church service. You made a promise to repay, and people of integrity honor their word regardless of the circumstances.

Something similar happened to me. I helped a fellow church member with an issue, and they promised to repay me on a certain date. Of course, it was more than $5. When the date came, I was expecting to be repaid. Instead, the church member told me that she sowed my money in the offering. If what she said was the truth, it would be another misplaced priority. You cannot give something that does not belong to you and expect to be blessed. Honor your commitments, and God will bless your integrity.

> "Agree with thine adversary quickly, whiles thou art in the way with him; lest at any time the adversary deliver thee to the judge, and the judge deliver thee to the officer, and thou be cast into prison."
> (Matthew 5:25 KJV)

When handling your creditors always be honest and truthful; they will respect you for it. If you are behind in your payments or something should happen that would result in you falling behind in your payments – you contact your creditors. Notice, I said you contact your creditors. Tell them what has happened to cause your payments to fall behind. Ask them to work with you. Have a plan to bring your balance current and discuss it with them. Then, do what you said you would do, faithfully and on time.

If you and your household experienced COVID and it caused a loss of income, which caused you to fall behind in your responsibilities, devise a plan of how to get back on track and talk with your creditors. Be open and honest. Ask them to work with you and let them know what you can do. Then do what you said you would do, faithfully and on time.

If your creditor does not agree with your plan but counters with their requirements, do not get mad. Thank them for their consideration. If you can truly agree to their proposal, then do so. But, if you cannot agree, tell them so, and agree to do your best. Never agree to something that you know you cannot do. It damages your credibility when you do not fulfill your word, resulting in your creditors no longer trusting you.

Creative Savings Strategies

> "But remember the Lord your God, for it is he who gives you the ability to produce wealth, and so confirms his covenant, which he swore to your ancestors, as it is today." *(Deuteronomy 8:18 NIV)*

It is always a good strategy to look for creative ways and opportunities to generate additional savings beyond the budget. A creative savings plan will not cost you anything but a little wisdom in application while providing extra dollars to help meet your savings goals.

Let's look at a few strategies easy to use:

- **The dollar bill challenge** – Every dollar bill you receive that the serial number begins with your initials (first/last name), you save. My husband and I made this into a game, and it was fun. We would place our bills in a box and, at the end of each month tally up the bills by initials. Whichever one of us acquired the most bills, the other would have to fulfill a pre-agreed chore of the winner. The chores would be doing the dishes for a week, cooking, sponsoring date night, etc. When we first began the challenge, we saved about $25 each. Wow, that was $50 extra dollars we deposited into our savings account. Then, as the months progressed and momentum began to build, our savings began to average about $40–$50 each. Now, that was an additional $80–$100 being deposited into our savings account beyond our monthly budget. Remember, we should always assign a goal to all our savings because it gives you purpose, and purpose will help you to stick to the plan and obtain the goal. We were planning a major trip to California for the following year. Therefore, we decided that our dollar challenge would be additional savings for our California trip. Once we made that decision, we were locked into the challenge. We even began buying our initials from our family and friends. When it was time for our California vacation, we had saved almost $1,000 from the dollar challenge.

- **Cash back promotions** – Many credit card companies and some debit card companies offer cash back promotions for using their cards. They often will have their own online shopping malls where the vendors will offer an additional cash back incentive to shop with them. Perhaps your credit card company may offer 1-2% cash back on every purchase you make. What this means is that every time you use your credit card, the company will give you 1-2% back. Should you shop in their online shopping mall, you gain even more in cash back. Each vendor will offer a cash back incentive when you buy from their company. The savings from these promotions can really add up. The challenge would be to make sure that you are a savvy credit card user. Being a savvy credit card user means that you manage your credit cards wisely, not charging more than you can afford to pay off monthly. We are moving more into a cashless society daily, and we are using credit/debit cards more than ever. So why not take advantage of the free money being made available to you? Free money? Yes, free money because you are going to make your purchase anyway. It only requires that we become more intentional when it comes to shopping. I tested this strategy. First, I identified vendors and/or vendor types that I buy from frequently. For example, drugstores. I looked for Walgreens, CVS, and online equivalent stores. Then, I made a list of the things I frequently buy from the drugstore. Then, I began to compare prices online versus in-store, including the cost of shipping/handling, and factoring in the cash back promotion. This lets me know what drugstore items I would purchase online. Big ticket items seemed to be more advantageous online from a cash back perspective. We purchased a new refrigerator. I shopped in person at the store, and when I found the desired refrigerator, I went online and made the purchase. This would net me $105 cash back (2% from the credit card company and 5% from the retail vendor).

- Note that online shopping malls consist of many of the same vendors you'd find in your local retail shopping malls.

- **Spare change (coins)** – This is another great savings strategy that would probably go unnoticed. At the end of each day, one simply empties their pockets or purse and places all loose coins in a jar or piggy bank. Once the jar or piggy bank is full, empty the contents and deposit them into a savings account. I am not a fan of having multiple full jars or canisters of coin throughout the house, because if a thief breaks into your home, your precious coin will be one of the first things they will carry out. Therefore, as you fill up a container- deposit the proceeds into a savings account. Saving your spare coin can be a fantastic way to help increase your emergency fund or help with upcoming household expenditures.

- **Business Marketing Promotions** – I am always a proponent of increasing your savings dollars by taking advantage of promotions that will pay you without costing you anything. Sometimes, companies will offer to pay you up to $25 for every friend you refer who uses their services. Some banks will pay you up to $300 to establish a bank account with them. If you find three bank promotions that will pay you up to $300 to open an account that offers zero to no bank fees, that's $900 you would be able to add to your savings or debt reduction. Business marketing promotion deals are all over and an excellent way to increase your revenue for additional savings or debt payoff.

- **Collecting pop bottles/cans for deposit** – I had a coworker who would collect pop bottles/cans and return them for the deposit to help finance his education. If he collected 50 cans per day, the deposit would be $5 per day/$25 per week, but over four weeks, he would have added $100 towards his education fund a month, and $1,200 in a year.

Chapter Four

Mitigating Outside Forces

"My people are destroyed for lack of knowledge. Because you have rejected knowledge, I also will reject you from being priest for Me; because you have forgotten the law of your God, I also will forget your children." *(Hosea 4:6 NKJV)*

There used to be a phrase or saying that if there was something you did not want a Black person to know, just write it in a book. A lack of knowledge is ignorance, and ignorance is not bliss. It is a force that has hindered and held our family captive in generational poverty. It is a force that must be dealt with to allow our families to thrive in the financial abundance that God intended.

We walk in generational poverty because we allow outside forces to rule and dictate our lives and the lives of our families. There is nothing that can disrupt a family's financial peace and prosperity more than the unexpected bringing them to financial disaster. The unexpected is an outside force that you cannot control, but property mitigation can help bring peace and prosperity to a family.

Outside forces, what outside forces?

"In those days Hezekiah [king of Judah] became sick and was at the point of death. And Isaiah the prophet, the son of Amoz, came to him and said, "For the Lord says this, set your house in order and prepare a will, for you shall die; you will not live." *(Isaiah 38:1 AMP)*

King Hezekiah was a prominent, successful, and wealthy man, who had a heart for God. God sent the prophet Isaiah to him, but instead of Isaiah bringing a message of healing and deliverance, he brought a message of death. God tells Hezekiah to prepare for his death because he was going to die.

Death is something that will befall all of us. No one is exempt. We all have an appointed time to leave this world. Unfortunately, no one knows when that will occur. Although, God forewarned Hezekiah that he was going to die. This is not always the case. No one knows when death will occur, so we must be ready to always leave here, with our houses in order.

There was a time in my marriage when my husband and I would not speak of death, as if the mere mention of dying would cause death to occur to one of us. Yet, we were Christians afraid of the "D" word.

When we accepted the Lord of Jesus as our Lord and Savior, our sins were atoned and covered by the blood of Jesus Christ. When we were immersed in the waters of baptism, we identified with the death, burial, and resurrection of Jesus Christ. We, in fact, died unto sin, and now we live our lives to the Glory and praise of God. It was through this that we no longer fear the "D" word.

Therefore, the first step to putting your house in order is getting your relationship with God in order. There is an order to everything, and if we want the divine flow in our lives, we must do things God's way.

Second, should you die today, how would your death affect your family? Would your family be able to thrive financially in your absence? Your income is now absent from the home, so how would your family survive? The ultimate gift a man or woman can give to their family is the gift of life insurance. Life insurance protects the family from financial disaster should the breadwinner of the family die prematurely (unexpectantly). It is not a get-rich source, but to replace that income that the family depended upon should that breadwinner die. Life insurance enables the family to maintain their standard of living. Without life insurance, the family can experience not only the loss of a loved one but the quick demise of the family itself.

One of my coworkers, who came from a family of eight, often testified how her dad did not believe in life insurance. When she was about seven, her father passed away, leaving her to mourn and suffer the consequences of his death, with her mother and seven siblings. She often talked about how poor they were and how, after her father's death, they were evicted from their family home. They would find themselves living in a two-bedroom apartment. She talked about how her mother would struggle to support them and make ends meet. She talked about holidays that were often nonexistent and the lack of support received from extended family. She talked about how her mother wished her father would have brought life insurance.

In another instance (outside force), a young woman gives birth to a beautiful baby boy. She and her child's father (boyfriend) were not married but committed to co-parenting their child. They had great hopes for the future, even the possibility of marriage. However, their dreams would soon be shattered; he was dead within thirty days. This death now placed all the financial responsibility on her in raising their child. He had no life insurance, and because of his limited time in the workforce, he had no social security benefits either.

In my introduction, I mentioned how my father would make comparisons between White and Black people. Most Caucasians, when a child is born or when pregnancy is announced, immediately secure that child's future by the parents getting life insurance on themselves. I have seen insurance purchased within the African American community, but too often, insurance is purchased on the child. Please note, should the child pass away, it may not cause a disruption to the family's financial future, but it may should the parent die.

In another instance (outside force), an unmarried couple, John Doe and Jane Not-Doe, considered themselves as a married couple without a marriage license. They shared two minor children together whose last names were Not-Doe. John was remarkably successful and wealthy. He did not believe in marriage, as it was only a piece of paper. It was only important that he and Jane loved one another. Their love would last ten years, but he died suddenly of a heart attack. John died without a will and no life insurance. Jane Not-Doe, his wife without a marriage license, would petition the court for her husband's estate. She was denied because they were not married. She was not his legal wife in the eyes of the law and God. As a result, Jane and her children were forced to leave the family home with no access to her "so-called" husband's financial assets.

The life this family would enjoy while John was alive would be no more. Why? Because of no official record of marriage. This common law syndrome, or "shacking up" as it's often called, usually ends with heartbreak and poverty. If there is life insurance, it's usually willed to "his" parents and not the mother of his children.

In another instance (outside force), during the civil rights movement, a prominent civil rights activist was blessed with a $1,000,000 life insurance policy, by a famous entertainer who recognized the trajectory the activist's life might succumb to. He wanted to make sure that the activist family was properly provided for. He believed that it would have been both an injustice, and a disgrace should this activist die and his family be forced to live like paupers and/or that a collection would be needed to be taken to raise funds for his burial. As a result, the activist family was able to thrive and live productive lifestyles in his death.

"Wisdom is the principal thing; therefore, get wisdom: and with all thy getting get understanding." *(Proverbs 4:7 KJV)*

In each of these outside forces scenarios, you see a common thread: how individuals allowed death to dictate their financial future. We know that death is real and will come to all of us. Life insurance is the vehicle to mitigate life's outside forces from wreaking havoc in our lives.

Outside Forces -The Insurance Review

Up to this point, we have discussed the need for life insurance. An outside force, if not properly managed, can wreak havoc on our financial future and our families. The same is true should you have life insurance. There can be outside forces working behind the scenes in your life insurance policies that can hinder your family, and without a proper review of your insurance, it will lie dormant until it explodes.

A proper insurance review seeks to make sure that your current policies are performing as they should, make needed corrections, and make any coverage adjustments if necessary. Note – All life insurance is not the same, and our need for life insurance changes as life happens. Life products change over time. Therefore, a life insurance policy purchased twenty or thirty years ago is well overdue for review.

When I grew up, it was during the time when insurance agents went door to door in neighborhoods selling life insurance. I remember the insurance people seemed to always be at my grandmother's home. They were writing policies, collecting premiums, and building professional relationships with the family. My grandmother was a woman who believed in life insurance: one, to provide for a proper burial and to leave something for her family. Not in a sense to make anyone rich, but to leave something behind for her family.

When my grandmother passed away, she had accumulated multiple small policies that she had paid for three and four times over, which in total was barely enough to pay for her burial. I was sad, angry, and hurt all at the same time because I felt that my grandmother had been exploited. I thought, all those years and all those agents, and no one thought to review her coverage. No one thought to update her insurance or even review it to see if she was in the right type of policies. The real answer to this question may never be known because both my grandmother and those agents are long gone.

I once reviewed the insurance coverage of a mother-daughter team. The mother had two small whole life policies for herself and her daughter. I think both policies were for $10,000. The daughter also had a $10,000 whole life policy, which she took out on herself seven years prior when she was pregnant with her second child. The daughter was very proud of the fact that she had life insurance. This appears to be great, but beneath the surface lies a possible imminent danger to this family. The question was, should I address it, or should I be like all the other agents they may have encountered and look the other way? I knew I had to address the issue because it was the right thing to do, and the Christ in me would not allow me to look the other way.

The daughter, although proud she is responsible for her own life insurance policy, is unaware that should she die, her family is not adequately protected. Yes, with a combined total of $20,000 in life insurance, her mother would be able to afford to bury her daughter and possibly have about $5,000 remaining from the two policies to raise her two granddaughters. Now, how far will $5,000 go in raising two minor grade school children? Not very far. Therefore, the quality of life this family currently enjoys is quietly at risk. Should the daughter pass away, the grandmother would be left with the responsibility of raising her grandchildren from her social security check. This would result in the impoverishment of this family, and many other negative things could await their future. The insurance review brought this matter to light, and the necessary changes were made to protect this family.

The insurance review can save the life of your policies. I remember reaching out to a client's spouse to secure a review appointment. She didn't have time to review his insurance. She thought the call was an attempt to sell her more life insurance. She felt our company was harassing her because other agents had reached out in the past requesting a review appointment.

Everything I said to her was met with resistance. She told me that her insurance company did not bother her, and that she had insurance with them for thirty years. My response was, "Your whole life has changed in thirty years." When I got tired of the debate, I told her okay, but one day you are going to wonder what happened, and I told her when that happens, please think back on this day when your husband's insurance company came knocking at your door. Then, she thought for a moment and quickly scheduled an appointment.

On appointment day, before I could review her husband's insurance, she had her insurance policies from the "other company" for me to review. It was discovered that her policies were about to explode and only had about two weeks of life remaining. When I say explode, I mean her insurance would terminate. It would no longer exist even though she had paid on it for thirty years. Please know that just because you are making your payments on time, like clockwork, does not mean everything is okay.

This next case is dear to my heart. I met a man who had purchased multiple policies for himself and his family. They were small policies but totaled to a sizable amount. When I sat to review with him and his wife, I discovered that there were multiple problems with each policy: incorrect spelling of names, social security numbers, beneficiaries, account owners... you name it, everything was wrong.

However, I was intrigued by the type of policies he purchased and how he put together his system or plan to protect his family. I invited him and his family to my office on a Saturday to address all the paper issues. It turned out to be a four-hour meeting of service paperwork, something that no other agent would have done. As agents, we are paid to sell life insurance.

But because of the magnitude of the problems, I could not see him getting the help, that he needed.

The problem was huge. Without the necessary corrections many of the policies would not have been paid out; there were so many of them his family would not even know where to begin. However, I was able to sort through all the paper and put everything in order. This client would die about a month later. I think of this family and know he can rest in peace, that his family was taken care of... no red tape, all smooth transactions.

Outside Forces – Powers of Attorney

My husband is thirty-five years my senior, and we have been married for thirty-two years. Throughout the years, we have had many friends and acquaintances who have gone home to be with God, but the circumstances surrounding their final demise in some cases were heart felt. Those who had their financial affairs in order had a greater handle or control of their financial future. Unfortunately, that was not so with others; they allowed outside forces to control their economic destinies, and that of their families.

I can recall while working on my master's degree, I was taking an estate planning class. I was fascinated by learning about wills, trust agreements, and powerful documents. I remember talking my grandmother into getting a medical power of attorney with the health care affidavit. The healthcare affidavit enabled my mother to talk with the doctors regarding my grandmother's care and treatment. The medical power of attorney gave my mother the ability to speak on my grandmother's behalf if she was unable. It allowed my mother to make medical decisions on her behalf in the event she was unable and/or no longer able to do so.

Little did I know that a year later, my mother would have to stand on those papers on behalf of my grandmother. My grandmother was sick and had been in the hospital for a couple days. One of the nurses who knew my grandmother called my mother to alert her that the doctors had my grandmother prepped for surgery without consulting anyone, and if she had those papers, she needed to come immediately to the hospital with them to stop it.

The doctors never consulted with my mother about operating on my grandmother. In fact, they said they did not have to because of HIPPA, but because of the medical power of attorney documents my grandmother had put into place, the doctors had to consult with my mother and allow my mother to make the decisions that she felt was in the best interest of my grandmother.

We must remember that doctors are only practicing medicine. Make sure that your family is empowered, so that they are not left helpless while doctors practice on you. It is necessary to have someone who has your best interest at heart to speak on your behalf, when you are unable to do so.

Please know this is not a senior thing; it is necessary for all adults. Did you know that when your child turns eighteen years of age, they are now an adult and covered under HIPPA law? What that means is that you, the parent, do not have the legal authority to speak on their behalf. So, just as these legal documents are needed for seniors, they are needed for your children and spouse. This is not something that should be put off because you feel you don't need it right now; because when you need these documents, it will be too late.

Having a family meeting and putting Medical Power of Attorney and Healthcare Affidavit documents in place can be a blessing and help to your family in crisis. It's a difficult thing to helplessly watch while trying to navigate the expensive court system on behalf of a loved one if you can financially afford to do so.

In Conclusion

The Bible says that my people are destroyed for lack of knowledge. Outside forces are the things that happen in life unexpectantly that can wreak havoc on the economic destiny of any family. Outside forces not properly protected against can keep a family poverty-stricken from one generation to the next.

Our grandparents understood that there was a need for life insurance, but unfortunately, many were sold a lie that all that was needed was insurance to pay for their burial; anything else would be an attempt to get rich.

We must understand that life insurance has been around almost since the beginning of time. Caucasians have utilized life insurance for decades to secure the thriving economic future of their families from generation to generation. Life insurance is to protect the family financially against the premature death of a loved one. Its purpose is to replace the income the family would lose. Life insurance is what has financially anchored and stabilized Caucasian families for generations.

We must not assume that everything is okay. A periodic review of your life insurance is necessary.

Chapter Five

Saving for College

"Behold, I will do a new thing; now it shall spring forth; shall ye not know it? I will even make a way in the wilderness, and rivers in the desert." *(Isaiah 43:19)*

I often think of the late entertainer Lou Rawls, a national spokesperson for the United Negro College Fund, and how he rallied the community to raise scholarship funds for African American students attending HBCUs (Historically Black Colleges and Universities). The commercial advertisement would show a Black woman scrubbing floors, and then you would hear the slogan, "A mind is a terrible thing to waste." It is unfortunate that with his passing, his telethon initiative was discontinued.

Parents today often have so many responsibilities that saving for college has been placed on the back burner. As a financial professional, I have seen parents wait until their children reach their junior and senior years of high school to begin thinking about the cost of higher education. They begin to seek grants and scholarships, only to learn they waited too late, and that government grants are no longer awarded like in the past.

When my nephew was about ten years old, I decided to invest in his future. My sister was a single mother with three children. At that time, I was a bank employee, working on my master's degree. I decided to start a college savings plan for my nephew by contributing $15 bi-weekly via payroll deduction, and increased contributions with every pay raise I received. Along the way, I would make additional bonus contributions.

When my nephew graduated from high school, he qualified to receive two football scholarships. However, due to an IRS situation, my sister would not complete the FAFSA application, resulting in my nephew not being able to take advantage of the scholarships nor receive any financial aid.

Fortunately, through this college savings plan, I was able to finance my nephew's first two years of college enabling him to obtain an associate degree. Thankfully, his mind was not wasted!

There is never an opportune time to begin saving for college. Selecting the right savings vehicle is crucial, and the earlier you begin the better.

Chapter Six

Creating Legacy

"A good man leaves an inheritance to his children's children." *(Proverbs 13:22 KJV)*

Oxford Language Dictionary

Legacy

1. an amount of money or property left to someone in a will.

2. the long-lasting impact of particular events, actions, etc. that took place in the past, or of a person's life.

One cannot establish a true purpose for life insurance outside of a death benefit for a funeral without knowing all the many benefits of life insurance. First, life insurance is not just about the funeral or a make someone rich scheme.

The true purpose of life insurance is to protect the family in the event of the death of the family's provider, also known as the "breadwinner." Without life insurance, the loss of the family's breadwinner can cause a lifetime of economic hardship and destitution for those family members who remain.

Life insurance can also offer us security when issues of life happen. For example, if you experience a change in your health and are diagnosed with a critical illness like cancer, heart attack, stroke, diabetes, etc., many new life policies have provisions to enable you to access policy funds to cover medical or household expenditures while you are living. This provision is not a loan but a provision of your policy. This can be a game changer for a family because most times, when someone experiences any of these illnesses, they are either unable to work on a steady basis or the illness disables them completely. This benefit can help prevent the depletion of financial assets and help maintain the family's sense of security.

There are three types of Life Insurance:

- Term Life is considered temporary insurance because it is sold for a duration of time. It is pure insurance, and the most inexpensive, especially in the early years. It does not build cash value. Offers temporary coverage for a duration of time. It is sold in 5-year increments ranging from 10-year policies up to 30-year policies. Most will allow the option to convert all or a portion of the coverage to whole life insurance before or at policy expiration. The policy face amount and premium remain constant throughout the life of the policy.

- Whole Life is permanent insurance designed to provide coverage for the life of the client, maturing at age 120 (older policies at age 100). There is no fluctuation in the policy face amount or premium; it remains the same throughout the life of the policy. This is an equity product because it builds in cash value, which is given to the policy owner upon surrender. The policy owner may borrow against the cash value without having to repay the loan, but the policy owner is expected to pay the annual interest on the loan. In the event of the client's death, the policy will payout the face amount of the policy less, any policy loans and accrued interest to the policy beneficiary.

- Universal Life/IUL is best defined by Investopedia as a type of permanent life insurance that, like other permanent insurance, has a cash value element and offers lifetime coverage if you pay your premiums. Unlike whole life insurance, universal life allows you to raise or lower your premiums within certain limits, and it can be cheaper than whole life coverage. However, if your investments underperform or you underpay for too long, it could affect your death benefit or cause your policy to lapse. Universal life products can be complex and subject to a higher degree of risk than Whole Life or Term insurance. The outside force here is that this product is not meant for everyone, and one should do their homework. Please let me say this again; this life insurance product is not for everyone, and care should be exercised.

The Beneficiary

The beneficiary is the person who has been designated by the policy owner to be the recipient of the life insurance funds when the insured dies.

Working in the financial services industry, I have seen both good and not-so-good. I have seen cases where people have willed entire life insurance policies to their pastors or close friends, and nothing to their families. I am sure this was probably done in good faith with the thought that their pastor or close friend would do right by their families, but with a lack of understanding that legally, the beneficiary is not required or obligated to share any of the life insurance proceeds with their family; and in many cases, they do not. Therefore, their family is left in the cold with no support.

While beneficiary selection is at the discretion of the person purchasing the product, I educate my clients on potential risks should beneficiaries be selected outside of what is considered normal, the family. However, should the client desire to have their pastor or close friend oversee and/or manage insurance monies for their family, there is a way to do so by establishing a family trust. I would recommend having a conversation with your pastor or close friend, share your concerns regarding your family, and ask for their help. Then, have an attorney draft the trust agreement naming the pastor or close friend as executor of the trust; then name the trust as the beneficiary of the insurance policy. This will protect your family, and both the reputation and integrity of your pastor and/or close friend.

In my opinion, I do think believers should leave a tithe to their church as a final offering in their death, should they desire to do so.

Policy Ownership

When taking out a life insurance policy on someone else, this could be a child, grandchild, significant other, etc. Please note that just because you are the official payor of the policy does not make you the legal owner of the policy. Also, ownership and beneficiary are different.

The beneficiary is the person who has been designated by the policy owner to be the recipient of the life insurance funds when the insured dies. The beneficiary has no other rights to the policy during the life of the insured. They cannot make any changes to the policy during the life of the insured. The beneficiary's only right is to file a death claim to obtain the proceeds of the policy at the death of the insured.

The person who owns the policy controls the policy. It's theirs, and they can make whatever changes they desire to it. What that means is that they can amend the beneficiary, liquidate policy cash value via loans and/or withdrawals, and even surrender.

Therefore, should you take out a new life insurance policy on the life of someone else, make sure the agent lists you as the owner of that policy on the insurance application, even if the agent says doing so will slow down the approval process. Insist that you are named the owner on the application anyway. A good agent will anticipate his underwriters' questions and address them appropriately within the application. This will help you avoid possible painful discrepancies in the future.

Consider this: you take out a life insurance policy on your son when he is seven, and you pay on that policy until he is age 42, with his own family and insurance. You decide you no longer need the policy and decide to surrender the policy (cash it in). You contact the insurance company, only to learn that they cannot discuss the policy with you because your son is the legal owner of the policy. You cannot make any changes, nor can you cash it in without your son's consent and signature, even though you paid the premiums for the last thirty-five years. How would that make you feel?

What if you learn that the policy you have been faithfully paying monthly premiums is suddenly terminated by the insurance company? You learn your son has drained all the cash value from the policy via withdrawals and policy loans without your knowledge. According to the insurance company, he was the legal owner of the policy, and it was his right to do so. How would that make you feel?

Now consider this: your son dies, and you are making plans for the funeral only to learn that you are NOT the beneficiary.

I cannot stress this enough: should you take a life insurance policy out on someone, and you will be the payor, make sure you are listed as the owner of the policy on the account application.

After the policy has been approved and issued, you will want to add a contingent owner to the policy. I recommend doing this immediately because should you die, the policy does not automatically revert to insured. It really becomes a part of your estate, but most times, no one knows about it, so the policy lies dormant until the cash value has been depleted, causing the policy to terminate.

The contingent owner will assume ownership of the policy at your death. In most cases, the insured should be named as the contingent, or a responsible person designated by you while you are alive.

Conclusion

Make sure that you tell your children about your life insurance policies, where to find them, what type of policies they are, and how they are being paid. If payment is being made electronically – tell them through what bank and when the payment comes out.

I know of a family that lost a $750,000 life insurance policy. The father became ill and went into a rehabilitation nursing facility. His payments were being maintained via bank draft from his bank account, but when his children decided to relocate him, they closed his bank account, which caused his insurance to lapse. No one knew about his insurance, nor checked his statements for automatic payments.

Appendices

Appendix-01

Statement of Financial Position
As of:_____

Assets – Part 1

Asset Type	Title	Value	Total
Cash	On Hand		
	Checking & Savings		
	CDs & Money Markets		
	Total Cash		
Investments	Stocks, Bonds, Mutual Funds etc		
	Retirement Accts		
	Annuities		
	Total Investments		
Receivables	Money Owed to You		
Real Estate	Primary Residence		
	Other Residence		
	Investment Property		
	Total Real Estate		
Personal Property	Automobiles		
	Boats		
	Furniture & Fixtures		
	Jewelry		
	Collections: Coin, etc		
	Other		
	Total Personal Property		
	Total Assets		

Statement of Financial Position

(Cont'd)

Liabilities & Net Worth – Part 2

Type	Title	Balance Due	Total
	Alimony/Child Support		
	Bank Loans		
	Credit Cards		
	Charitable Pledges		
Liabilities	Installment Debt (Automobile)		
	Insurance Policy Loans		
	Mortgage, Primary Residence		
	Mortgage, Other Residence		
	Personal Loans		
	Student Loans		
	Other: Unpaid Bills		
	Total Liabilities		
	Net Worth		
	Total Liabilities & Net Worth		

Appendix-02

Personal Statement of Cash Flows
For the month of:_____

Income - Part 1

Type	Title	Amount	Total
Income	Employment		
	Salary & Wages, Net		
	Commissions		
	Bonuses		
	Other		
	Total Employment Income		
Income	Investments		
	Interest		
	Dividends		
	Net Rental Income		
	Business Income		
	Annuities		
	Social Security Benefits		
	Pension/Retirement Plan		
	Other		
	Total Investment Income		
Income	Miscellaneous		
	Inheritances		
	Alimony		
	Child Support		
	Other		
	Total Miscellaneous Income		
	Total Inflows Available for Expenses		

Personal Statement of Cash Flows (Cont'd)

Expenses – Part 2

Type	Title	Amount	Total
	Ordinary Living Expenses		
	Food		
	Clothing		
	Childcare		
	Entertainment		
	Household		
	Medical		
	Transportation		
	Utilities		
	Charitable Contributions		
	Total Ordinary Living Expenses		
Expenses	*Debt Payments*		
	Credit Card Payment, Principal		
	Credit Card Payment, Interest		
	Auto Loan Payment, Principal		
	Auto Loan Payment, Interest		
	Mortgage Payment, Principal		
	Mortgage Payment, Interest		
	Total Debt Payments		
	Insurance Premiums		
	Auto Insurance Premiums		
	Disability Insurance Premiums		
	Homeowners Insurance Premiums		
	Life Insurance Premiums		
	Medical Insurance Premiums		
	Total Insurance Premiums		

Personal Statement of Cash Flows (Cont'd)

Expenses – Part 3

Type	Title	Amount	Total
Expenses	**Tuition and Education Expenses**		
	Taxes		
	Federal Income Tax		
	State & City Income Tax		
	FICA		
	Property Tax (Residence)		
	Total Taxes		
	Total Expenses		
	Discretionary Cash Flow		

Appendix-03

Debt Payment Ledger

Creditor's Name: ─────────────────────

Address: ─────────────────────

─────────────────────

Telephone No: ─────────────────────

Account No: ─────────────────────

Date	Description	Debit (+)	Credit (-)	Balance
	Beginning Balance	-	-	$

Comments:

─────────────────────
─────────────────────
─────────────────────
─────────────────────

About the Author

Cherl L. Robinson, MSFS (Cherl – without "y"), is a financial professional in the Michigan metropolitan Detroit area. She enjoys working with educators, professionals, small business owners, and their families helping them to become properly protected, debt-free, and achieve financial independence while building generational wealth.

Cherl Robinson has worked in the financial services industry for over ten years. She holds a master's degree in finance, specializing in personal financial planning from Walsh College and a bachelor's degree in business administration, specializing in financial management.

Before starting her financial service business, Cherl worked in the banking industry in commercial credit for over twenty years. She developed and taught biblical Christian stewardship in her local church. Professionally, she offers various financials services, including, life insurance, retirement strategies, and employee benefits. Cherl may be reached via email at cherl.robinson@financegodsway.com.

www.ingramcontent.com/pod-product-compliance
Lightning Source LLC
Chambersburg PA
CBHW060427090426
42734CB00011B/2474

9781953788986